A Festivity of Love
2

A Festivity of Love

2

More Poems
from St Endellion

Edited by

Judith Pollinger and

Paul S. Fiddes

Firedint Publishing Oxford

In Memory of Kate (1971-2016)

How devastated was I when I lost you?
(You would have said it was careless of me.)
Nothing can describe my feelings seeing you
lying lifeless in the ditch
on a July morning.
The sun had gone out of our lives, we were bereft,
empty and lost.
So, what are we left with?
A huge hole in our lives, a massive pit of despair.
But we must move on and feed on the memories
she left us with.
The smiles, laughter and love she gave to us
and all those she met.
We must slowly begin to fill that pit with memories
that no one can take away.
When we look into the night sky,
the brightest star shining down on us will be Kate.

- Kate's mother, Frances Kent

Preface

This volume is the second collection of poems about love to be launched at a North Cornwall Book Festival held at St Endellion. The first, also entitled *A Festivity of Love*, appeared in 2019. As in the previous volume, not all the writers are from North Cornwall, but all have a connection in some way with the Collegiate Church of St Endellion, or with 'Endelienta', a charitable association for music, literature, art and spirituality associated with the church. A number are members of the St Endellion Poetry Group.

Almost all the poems included here are previously unpublished. They come from writers who are published poets, from prize-winning poets, and from amateur poets. They are contributed by those who compose regularly and from those who do so occasionally. They range widely over the theme of love, including love of nature, love for partners, present and lost, and—in a landscape full of churches named after Cornish saints— love of God. At a time of climate crisis when human beings are bent on destroying their environment, it is significant that many of the poets cannot separate their love for another person from their empathy with the whole natural world.

The editors are especially grateful to the poets Maggie Mealy and Chris Woods who have assisted with the selection of poetry for the volume.

Acknowledgements

'The Reservoirs of Denshaw' by Chris Woods, from *Orbis* Magazine, Summer 2022; 'The Perfect Couple' from *Recovery* by Chris Woods ©Enitharmon Press 1997; 'Green' by Chris Woods ©The London Magazine, September 2014.

'Porch' from *The Lost Boys* by Victoria Field ©Waterloo Press 2013; 'A Woman who Looks on Glass' from *Many Waters* by Victoria Field ©Fal Publications 2006.

'Honourable Estate' by Kate Compston, from *Together: Marsden the Poetry Village Anthology* ©2019 Write Out Loud.

A FESTIVITY OF LOVE 2

Kate Compston

Carrying Osip Mandelstam

I must keep moving, always
one step ahead of my pursuers.
I hold him still

within the circular needles
of my ribcage,
his stitches patterning

my heart and lungs,
the colours of him
vibrant to me, invisible

elsewhere. I mustn't slip
a stitch of him, no
slackening. I speak him

every moment, under
my breath. He has become
my breath, his rhythms

invigorate my blood.
If caught, I die;
he dies a second death.

*

I have a second fear:
if I survive this Terror,

open my chest wall, let
his words fly free,

will I unravel?

The Russian poet, Osip Mandelstam, was imprisoned for his writing during the Stalinist repression. He died en route to the Siberian gulag in a transit camp. His widow, Nadezhda (the name means 'Hope') memorized his unpublished work, and lived a nomadic life, evading arrest herself. Many years later, she was able to publish Osip's work.

A FESTIVITY OF LOVE 2

Honourable Estate

Daniel Trewithen, jacket-lining dipped,
half-mast, under his threadbare tweed;
rolled trousers, hosting crumbs of soil
and burrs, like keloid wounds.

Hilda (née Cottle), blue apron mapped
with gravy islands; once-wild head
grey haired – recalcitrant wire-wool
still springing out of bounds.

They stumble round their garden, slipped
beyond neatness, grunt at bolted chard
they'll be hard-pushed to pull.
Husband, wife – each tends

the other more than their small plot; wrapped
in quietness, not much to be said –
not now; their conversation in the braille
of calluses, clasped hands.

A FESTIVITY OF LOVE 2

Not This Time

Next time, if there is a next, if *next*
has any meaning in what comes afterwards,
the train will arrive on time.

The wild anemones will be blowing
on the bank, there'll be the scent of rosemary;
you will be waiting still.

Next time, there will be no screaming
in the dark of tunnel or mind,
no screeching of brakes,

no bland announcement saying nothing,
except what's obvious: *there was an incident...*
Next time, there will be petals

falling to the ground, not ash, nor tears.
Next time, we'll not fail to meet; we'll move
towards each other, as in fantasy

and films, with grace of dancers so well versed
we can forget technique. Can there be a *next*?
If so, let it begin ...

A FESTIVITY OF LOVE 2

Explorers

She took her enquiring eye
into the museum of memories,
sifted through exhibits: locks
of hair, sketches,
a telegram, black-edged.

He took his enquiring ear
into a forest of fearings:
water gushing in deep-pile
darkness, the cry
of a child.

She took her enquiring hands
into a house of music.
She entered its core, touched
keys and strings. She touched
her own throat.

He took his enquiring tongue
into windways of weather;
he sought the taste of mist,
gradations of snow, deluges,
sun on a ledge.

They took their expanding hearts
into tentative embraces,
rehearsed each other's
wounds. Wept. Brushed each scar
with ointment, kisses.

Yvonne Dean

Tehidy a Piece of Heavens

You have to lift your eyes in this place,
For unfettered expansion.
Your chin goes up – head back, not too close,
in case you swoon
at the majesty.
Of trees.

You imagine swooping like the birds,
through perfumed gaps of air.
Parachuting willow seeds,
float in sunshine
on a breeze.
Woodpigeon croo - croo,
Chiff chaff, black bird song,
butterfly dance.

A FESTIVITY OF LOVE 2

Song of the wayside

Paradise is around the corner,
it happens several times a day.

During a walk to the letter-box
up the same old road. Out of a wall
a fox glove, inside small dots of black
on pink finger caps, ascend in size...

Around the same old corner – there
in the gray stony gutter, a delicate
violet in flower, giving brief utter joy...
A burst of yellow from a hedge
where sparrows chatter all at once.

Past the same old bus stop, sits
a red letterbox, at its back between
it and the fence a fern is uncoiling,
in order to release feathery fronds.

Sudden sunshine bathing all.

Vicky Edwards

Don't Fill My Heart

Love of mine –
Don't fill my heart
When I lie at night asleep
Then come morning
Slip away
And as I'm waking
Leave a boulder buried deep.

Heart

Heaving heart
That hangs in half
In branches high
Swinging back and forth
I hear it cry
Lonely in the night
It sings a mournful lullaby
And as I watch it swinging
Through my tears
I wave goodbye

Beauty –

For me
Is in the smallest things of all

A breath before
The touch of skin on skin
Holding life still for a moment

A sparkle glinting in a stream
A summer evening's hillside
Lit by a moonbeam

What do you find beauty in?

Are you brought to stillness
On a woodland walk at dawn
Where clear notes of birdsong
Dance high above
The rusty leaves' crackle?

Does the grace of the tall trees in silent chorus swaying
Magic you to stand and stare, like me?

A harmony so perfect
So poignant, it accompanies a tear
Slipping in slow motion
Down your cheek?

And have you ever marvelled
At the contours of a pure-white pebble
So hard, so round, so smooth
Held it in your hand

A FESTIVITY OF LOVE 2

And turned it over and over
To absorb its silken surface?

Then you are, like me, a lover
Of the smallest things of all.

Paul S. Fiddes

The Phoenix

Straight from the sun he dropped into our world,
dancer of Stravinsky's measures, lover
of Shakespeare's faithful dove, his wings unfurled
endlessly renewed from fire his mother.
Christ-symbol, incandescent in earth's clime,
but now, submerged in planet-warming time
the life-provoking gap twixt earth and fire
near-lost, collapses on his funeral pyre.

And is this too the lot of love for you
no longer to be reborn in worlds to come?
Will all our converse have no image true
our mutual moments have no glorious sum?
No: one phoenix holds all loving in his flame,
unextinguished it remains, through death the same.

The Griffin

Twice-blessed beast, actor of air and earth,
golden in grace and fleet of lion-limb,
tail and talons in baffling movement mixed,
ah! *Domine deus*, keeper of hidden hoard,
field-folded treasure, no less loot of love!
Blended were body and air ages ago,
enfolded in a field, clasped in a kiss,
we two drawing deep breath from us both,
thrilling throughout, never stirring to stop.
On our sea-sculpted cliff the wind of his wings
was within us, ours his sinewy strength,
heaving to Dante's heaven cupid's car.

This we rightly remember, O Lord of love.

*This poem reflects Dante's account of the fabulous beast, the
Griffin, in Purgatorio, Canto 29, and – as suited to its subject –
uses the alliterative scheme of Anglo-Saxon poetry.*

A FESTIVITY OF LOVE 2

Victoria Field

Kitchen
for Tamara Jones

five dinner plates, white with blue patterns
love their arrangement on the table

the green plate with its decoration of birds
holds the frittata blissfully

grapes, strawberries, blueberries, raspberries
have an end of summer song and sing it sweetly

cheese smoked on the Roseland is some way
from the French cheese oozing its aromas
but they both delight in being cheese

rosemary bread is prickly and oily
we need that too

someone's brought 'herring in fur coats'
gleaming beetroot, merry spring onion

at one with the 'salat iz crabov' – all claws
and cold water Northernness

oh, and there's bits of this and that
frivolous spirals of pasta, pureed apples
in floral tea cups, one saying 'Mother'

and it's all part of our laughter
our womanish talk, our love for each other.

A FESTIVITY OF LOVE 2

Icon Painter

I want to dazzle you
with pigment

fish glue
to swim you towards me
filling the water with lapis

egg yolk
from visions of rings in shop windows

I add rice glue
billions of hearts beating in China
ache with my missing you

egg white
harvest of love from the sheets

They say bone glue and marble
give permanence
my spent flesh is cold with not touching you

Give me some rabbit glue
You lollop over lush fields
faster and faster

How can I catch you?
Bind you in three hundred shades of green?

Porch
after R.S. Thomas

How close do you feel to God?
asks the priest. As I sit with my back
to the altar, God answers for me,
throws open the locked door

of my heart, turns the heavy ring
of the handle, lifts the stiff catch,
takes away my breath on the swing
of smooth hinges, lets in the air

that is everywhere. God isn't arriving
nor leaving, through this four-chambered
porch under my ribs. He is the opening
and the door, the push and pulse

of whatever moves through me,
the whole red messiness of love.

A Woman Who Looks on Glass

In the last year of her life
she blew an unexpected legacy
on a vast picture window
for Cedarwood, the bungalow
where they celebrated
not quite sixty years of marriage,
sat watching Blackie and the other birds
diving for fat, nuts and cake, looking
for the old man in blue overalls
leaning on his rake in the lettuce lines
who wouldn't be in for his tea.

A FESTIVITY OF LOVE 2

Craig Marshall

Ecstasy in a Daydream

I will say it with words, I will show you by touch.
Never too little but maybe too much.
The poems I'll write and the looks I will throw
Are simply expressions of something you know.

The climaxing rush of the waves on the beach
The breeze that caresses the trees in its reach.
The mountains that contour the blue of the sky,
Are raptures I sense in the breath of your sigh.

The rhythms and beats of our hearts are as one;
A harmony something together we've won.
I know that our souls have been dancing together,
A joy they have promised to keep up forever.

When I'm not with you and life's drained of colour
When days seem less vibrant or empty and duller.
I'll daydream my way to your eyes and your smile,
And remember your passionate touch for a while.

And blessed by the bliss of that momentary trance
My body will sing and my spirit will dance.
And standing quite still by the statue of time
I'll open myself to these feelings sublime.

And in that still moment of ecstatic embrace
I'll breathe in your hair and I'll cradle your face.
And whether I'm with you, without you, above you
I'll know that for certain, forever I'll love you.

A FESTIVITY OF LOVE 2

John May

Vacancy: Marriage Counsellor

`Lord, thou hast poured me out and curdled me.'
Yes, but I am going to climb back over the rim.
Look! I appreciate the unremitting pace of History
and that dreams are not to be replayed on mere whims,
and yet I guess that paradise is an end as well as a start.
I certainly feel well cheesed off out here, and I kick my heels
and frown and fail to sit still and I stamp my heart
and I must tell her what my miserable soul feels:
"My dear Eve, I know I sold you down the river
over the fruit thing, but do you ever think of me,
and in dark hours, with a raging unspent fire, quiver?
In this large labouring land of thistles I have to see you.
`I am like an owl in the wilderness.'
I am lonely, weak, was wrong, want your only tenderness."

The quotes in italics are from Job 10.10 and Psalm 102.6.

Extraction

My darling,
I would like to extract you from the kitchen
and place you in your dreams.
You would be entirely forgiven for thinking
"Why doesn't this nitwit just take me away
I could do with a day at the seaside,
I would like to buy a new dress
without worrying about money?"

This is what artists, painters, have always done,
locating the virgin and child not in a mangy stable
tired and poor and unloved after a long journey,
but gorgeous in some vestibule of eternal glory;
finding the farmer's boy with a red waistcoat
lapping water from a pool by a glorious cornfield
instead of thirsty in a muddy ditch;
giving the king's mistress perfect breasts
instead of – well, Agnes, perhaps she did have,
one at any rate, Sorrel that is,
I never saw the other myself.

I would like to place you in dreams
of such quixotic beauty
that for a moment you would escape
the constant demands, responsibilities
and plain hard work, that sense of duty and the
unremitting labours of each day.
And I promise to help a bit more
with the dusting, washing, cooking,

A FESTIVITY OF LOVE 2

earning, caring, mending, ironing,
peacekeeping, and... and...
and I will clean the bathroom and the loo.

But first I will find you some dreams.

Menu Complet 45F

Assiette apéritive

In their twenties they enjoyed love à la carte
his gamey bird, her hot chilli tarte,
unsure of what the items on the menu meant,
longing, frightened, shy, fierce on the scent,
sniffing the wind, sheer naked sex,
c'est pas tout 'dans le texte'.
They also talked through the night
about art and literature like bright
young things. Their eyes as full of dreams
as apple blossom shaken by a breeze.
Starlight!

A FESTIVITY OF LOVE 2

Soupe

Then they were married and landed in the soup.
We do that when we want this love to last for ever;
and then there's the general conspiracy of Granny,
religion, Victorianism, and tax benefits if we're canny.
We are political animals and commit to the group;
first couples, then families, broods, tribes, all forming
fatherlands and filling Mother Earth,
for better, for worse; for richer, for poorer;
in sickness and in health... this union
knotted forever, or at least til I bore her
to death. But come! That's not the right spirit,
is it? We used to believe that a vow
was unbreakable, and in the pageants
of mediaeval courtesie, if not now,
it can never be broken: my word is my bond,
my signature in the registers is me,
the extension of my own right hand.
My loyal allegiance is there for all to see.
Devotion! Acceptance! Expectations? Panic!
Wonder.

Plat du Jour

They might be a skewered kebab and a lame duck,
mais cette tarte de mariage est donc cuite au feu,
in labour, in tolerance, self-giving and hard work:
a good partnership is like silver refined in the fire.
It is a grand vol-au-vent with a thousand rolling layers,
creative, patient, spiritual, fulfilling, aspiring, sharing,
a mille feuille of all the years of smiles and tears,
supporting, giving space, shaping, embracing, caring,

with deep love and laughter, fun and holding hands,
and perhaps misunderstandings, provocations, rows,
silence.

Dessert

It's a fine thing to find your lover is the truest friend
you have. Trifles and jam roly-polies don't have to end
but they enjoy sorbets on long hot summer days.
The damson and apple tansy pudding they share:
it's harvest time, their children are up and away,
and then the days draw in and they enjoy those rare
and precious times of trusty friendship,
quiche reine-claude, blackberry swiss charlotte,
hedgerow fare, the simple made best of all,
most true.

Fromage

In the last sunshine of a late summer day
they sit on a bench in a quiet Parisian square,
a few figs to nibble with their pain ficelle and Valençay.
Holding hands no words are spoken, but as in prayer
they commune in a silent understanding
and harmony of souls. The branching
plane trees overarch them. In wonder
passers-by stop to consider this rapture
that is so complete. Then they wander
slowly home. No words of mine can capture
this warmth.

A FESTIVITY OF LOVE 2

Port

Now that the claret days are done,
finding their lives and hearts are one,
they slip their moorings one still winter day
and drift beyond us, castaways
to Love.

Sur le Terasse

Afterwards, the meal finished, we all go out onto the terrace.
We muse and talk together, dawdling and dreaming in the
musky candlelight. Looking upwards through the cherry
blossom and beyond the dusky, starry sky we see them once
more, still holding hands, where long ago they were before.
Heaven.

*Some of the image of the couple on the bench in the first half of
`Fromage' is inspired by an article or essay I read in Glastonbury
Abbey Retreat House in about 1992, perhaps by Michael
Paternoster.*

A FESTIVITY OF LOVE 2

Maggie Mealy

Expectations

I was a long way from home,
in a new home but detached
from expectations of homeliness.

I knew it would be a struggle, less money
for everything, less time for nights at wine bars,
restaurants, theatres, parties.

And then it started – the tap on the door,
the neighbour with a tiny tissue-wrapped package,
the strange parcels in the post from relatives whose names
I hardly knew, the hand-me-downs from seldom-met-with-
    friends;
"maybe you'll find a use for these", the hand-made garment
    from
a stuttering distant-colleague; "I marched for the right of a
    woman
to choose, but find only love and hope for every newborn
    child."

As I grew larger I fell away from the familiar yet felt held,
    closer
to those who had been distant, began to get an inkling that,
    not just
my body was changing; the contours of my world
had shifted, would never again
be the same.

A FESTIVITY OF LOVE 2

I was *expecting*, but
not this.

A FESTIVITY OF LOVE 2

Moon music for new mothers

Forget what you have read, erase words
as you know them, leave your voice until
morning, enter the world of the little one,
she who howls if you leave her, she who
howls if you don't; yes, her pain is yours
now and you can bear it.

                    Dim the harsh light,
look to the moon, the white-faced-one who hovers;
you both are in her arms.

                    Relax into the contours
of night, the cool of the room.

                    Let your body sway
to an internal music, your heartbeat calm
to a steady beat.

                    A lullaby is deep inside you,
all sound, no prescribed words, first sung
by Eve, maybe, but a gift to pass on, there
for all mothers when they need it.

        You will get through this,
and she will, too,
  and she will, too,
     and she will, too.

A FESTIVITY OF LOVE 2

The idea of return

The idea of return is a strange one; we are not mail-order items which, if a poor fit, can be returned.

Once a work colleague told me not to worry if I miscarried – the spirit of my child would return to God, return to me when my life was ready.

She was a strange one (this colleague), unpopular because she was hugely fat (never an asset, even in the 70's), a Christian who talked about God (frequently) and her Pastor (more frequently) and neither subject endeared her to us. Also, she was a Single Mother (back then this was said with Capital Letters).

On my last lunch time (I was about to go on maternity leave) she asked if we minded her practising her piece for the Church Social. She ate her egg sandwich in record time, stood up and sang "Smile, though your heart is aching".

It seemed to me that the whole office lifted, filled with light, was transformed.

I was a temp and finished my pregnancy at home, had a daughter whose spirit came with her direct (never needed to be returned to God) and whom I never wished to send back.

I never returned to that office, never found out if my colleague was still beautiful.

A FESTIVITY OF LOVE 2

Jane Newberry

Call Me Ungracious

Can I just say these are
Ecuadorian roses ... and the
Interflora man delivered his
lecture on flower care as
madness welled up inside.

Wish I was quicker, I'd have
re-directed the ludicrous
ensemble to the old folks home –
but I'm slow and sad and
just feel how much I miss you.

There's no link of any kind
between you and Ecuadorian roses.
Perhaps they are embarrassed by
their carbon footprint? – They should be,
and the excess cellophane and the

message, "this gift has been
hand created by Kathkyn ...
lovingly prepared ..." but I
don't want Kathkyn's synthetic love,
I want you, with your returning embrace.

A FESTIVITY OF LOVE 2

Dead Robin

Curtains drawn across a far-off window
as she said it –
Robin died; didn't you know?

And it came back to me in jerky snatches,
like an old movie . . .
showing me the rabbits

and admiring his woodwork
for the cage, trying not to stare
at his tanned face

and bright blue eyes. –
was he really that beautiful?
"boys are not beautiful . . .

they may be handsome",
she told me with disapproval
and that rebuff fuelled the thrill

of being in the boat with
no grown-ups, only Shandy,
his dog whom I loved too.

Jersey full of hay seeds,
woolly hat crammed on in August
and enviable baseball boots

whose soles I followed
in the straw-stack darkness
and was punished later

for such a foolish stunt.
"You could have been killed"

. . . and would have died for love.

A FESTIVITY OF LOVE 2

All the Ways of Being Sorry

I cannot take back the words
but only dilute the hurt.
Guilt aches deeper
than the first wound.
I bring you the tendrils,
tendresse and little salad leaves
from the garden,
the first plump gooseberries,
their sharp sarcasm
sweetened by so much sugar.
I bring quails' eggs
cooked with exquisite care,
hoping the peeling breaks
the shell of silence.
Casting my message into the sea
in the arc of a thrown pebble,
I look to see if
your patch of sky
is rippled by the closeness
of my sigh.

A FESTIVITY OF LOVE 2

David Penhale

At Trerice

Returning to this old house again
has caught me off-guard.
Some magician has drawn back a curtain
on this Tudor miniature
with its manicured lawns,
patient parterre and neat knot-garden,
everything straight lines and formal greetings.
It sits on its plot
like a perfect toy
a doll's house containing
centuries of secrets.
I step inside the granite doorway
from fifteen-hundred and seventy-two
slip
between a crack
in the worlds
before any hint of a civil war
to a time when parents and children
whoop, and laugh together at the sky
play at families in fusty old clothes
drawn like familiars from the cupboard
they set-to games in the long gallery
under the gaze of landowners, slavers,
adventurers and poets, as kayles are bashed
(each 'town' knocked down 'in a rush'!)
and through the oriel
a familiar family is whooping
and laughing
down the years, rich in

A FESTIVITY OF LOVE 2

meadowsweet, stitchwort,
pink campions
with the world
entire
in their eyes.

Judith Pollinger

Love

You were sound, solid, stable,
dependable, consistent, sure,
like a plain wooden bench or table.

Your love was shown in practical ways,
making, mending, restoring,
in a simple, ordinary succession of days.

I craved overt expressions of love, but soon learned
there'd be no surprise gifts, cards or flowers,
none of the tokens for which I yearned.

On our wedding eve, I eagerly opened the note
you'd sent, expecting words of undying love;
'Make sure you polish your shoes', you wrote.

Torn between laughter and tears, I tucked it away,
wondering what life would be like
on the farm, after the wedding day.

More blunt notes followed: 'Ring the vet before ten,
open the barn, collect the eggs, check on the calves,
prepare harvest tea today for twelve men'.

And the Valentine card each year I longed to see?
When questioned, you'd answer, 'But why?
There's no point, you'd know it was me'.

A FESTIVITY OF LOVE 2

Forty years wed, we went for a few days away,
staying with friends on the Scillies,
watching the sea birds, walking for miles each day.

Sea a shimmering blue, sun high in the sky
I went for a swim; returning I found a note
formed from pebbles and shells, 'I. L. Y.'

A FESTIVITY OF LOVE 2

Love and Loss

I

After the great event
when you had gone,
never to return,
you had not gone.

Still fitted against you, I lay
held in the curve of your body,
your skin against mine;
knowing the hand held warmly in yours,
was not my hand holding my own.

Slowly you withdrew,
as though you knew
I could make my way without you.

II

I dare to open the wardrobe,
see hanging there
your shirts and suits and ties.

I reach for the jacket
you often wore,
with its worn collar, sagging pockets.

I clutch it to me,
breathe in the lingering scent
still faintly present.

A FESTIVITY OF LOVE 2

III

Forget-me nots,
your favourite flower,
blue as your eyes;
I asked the florist for them
for your funeral,
then found them in our garden.
I placed a posy on your coffin,
and year by year
I lay them on your grave.

Today I found them growing there.

A FESTIVITY OF LOVE 2

The Old Coat

Each Spring I think
I really will throw out
 that old grey coat.

Then Summer comes
and still it hangs, limp and listless,
one pocket torn.

A frosty Autumn day
and once again I put it on,
find warmth and comfort.

You died in winter.
not waiting till I reached you;
so I wear your coat, feel you still near.

Michael Spinks

Grace

'Who straight, Your suit is granted, said, and died,' so willing
us
      the land on which the treasure lies,
            this shifting form of love.

Grace is a sail on a cavernous,
            overwhelming sea,
    The scorching spray of despair.
Grace is the warm, warm body
         of the once dead Lord.
Grace is love's fruit, justice
         its earlier bloom of flower.
Grace is the wolf who stalks and kills,
         devours its quivering prey,
The sparrowhawk who leaves as evidence
    A scattered cross
         of feathers on the lawn.
Grace is the touch upon the forehead, and inside
         all the sockets of the heart.
Grace is the thunderclap that precedes striking rain,
    The flagrant fire that showers bursts of pain,
The sudden fall of jagged ice, the shape of beauty,
    Grace is the path between dark trees.
Its declaration, its emanation, there,
         a tear run down the face of God.

A FESTIVITY OF LOVE 2

He for she

He for she, and
conversely, she for he;
reply, rejoin, repay, initiate,
begin, and move.
The walkers observe
the plaintive sweetness
of what grows between,
their feet an intrication
across the polished space,
a dance of hopefulness.
The sculptors define an essence,
nobility and intricacy,
distinct and private mouldings.
He, the man, is block,
all outward pressing, air
stressed with pulse and sight.
Convex at every face,
the surface curved towards,
urgent and instant, present.
She, the female, whirl
of inner stasis,
ingrown secrets shared
carefully, responsibly and once.
Concave at heart,
urgent, insistent, responsive.
Each moves out from central space,
expanding, he; she centripetal,
confluent, attractive, outward, inviting.
Those hollows evident and shared,
in his are cavities, spaces into,
explorations and revealings,

A FESTIVITY OF LOVE 2

depths and showings across
and joining opposite surfaces,
interior workings.
In hers, what is touchable is emanation
around and out of hidden interiority,
circles body and surround
the attraction of space,
blood's interior machinery.
Beauty and meaning have shape
and each will have
a mirrored heart of recognition.
See them exhibited side by side:
complete incomplete, a pairing of hemispheres.
The pianist ends and closes and so departs –
The voice of music speaks on.
Each of us is a pierced form.

Paul Temme

Mending a Corpse

The search for the box
with the photos seems a waste
but I go on, like a drunk
finding his way home.

Take my picture?
I did.
You, by a laurel,
in pearl, cream and grey,
fearless of the lens.
I crave the image though
it terrifies and torments.
Whips my mind.

In attic dark
I hunt the past but
I am careless with things.
Friends.
Lovers.
You.
Always have been.

A FESTIVITY OF LOVE 2

Blue-black

Blue-black runs from the pen you gave me,
inked imaginings of you not here; like
an unrisen moon, leaving only stars
as guides to a map-less universe,
and no companion for the soaking dark.

Beneath Us are the Bodies of Saxons

Beneath us are the bodies of Saxons,
lords in longboats, revealed in August droughts.

We sail through time towards late afternoon,
when dry earth crumbles between fingertips.

The sea-washed blue of your summer dress
matches your eyes and is unbearable.

It billows, trapping the immodest breeze.
My breath slows. I harvest a memory

of hair the colour of corn. From the land
our tree towers, a mast rigged in green,

we lean on its fissured bark under a
loaded sky but I come without treasure;

no field flowers nor anything carved from
wood. So, at dusk, under the pinprick of

Venus, I will pillage the hedgerow for
dog rose and campion and bind them with

honeysuckle vines as my parting gift.
All lovers have this unsweetened moment.

A FESTIVITY OF LOVE 2

Fay Warne

Love

Look
On the
Virgin,
Emmanuel

A FESTIVITY OF LOVE 2

Rowan Williams

Herr, dein Mitleid: **duet**
(For the St Endellion Festival community, and in joyful
memory of Fran Hickox)

They smile; their skins are glistening and flushed,
breath on its way back to normal. They have been
where you long hungrily for what you have
and have all you are hungry for, and the fast
shuttle ties you in a bristling weave
of air, skin, sweat. Last night was rough
for him, a glass or three too many and a pointless
row with the new girlfriend. This afternoon
she had a bad phone call with her father in the Home,
then fell into the pit of dread about
her weight. They seldom meet, are mildly
polite, respectful(ish), grumbling a little
over the session rates, sharing raised eyebrows
at a neighbour's slip, determined not to let go

Of one another as they throw their fishing lines
across the dark, and watch, still after years amazed,
the clicking into place that holds the pull of those
black pendulums hung from the wires. They drag
deep at each others' breath, raise the goosebumps
and beads of sweat out of each others' skin, their eyes
shine and they smile, these tired casual strangers,
calling to one another over the swollen brook
of sound, not to forget they are accompanied,
absolved. They roll apart out of the chaste
and blazing bed of *Mitleid, Erbarmen*,

A FESTIVITY OF LOVE 2

smile and dry their faces, having been
in love. And sit down carefully beside
the other hungry acrobats.

*The title of this poem refers to a duet from the Christmas
Oratorio by J.S. Bach, beginning 'Herr, dein Mitleid, dein
Erbarmen' ('Lord, your compassion, your mercy').*

Chris Woods

Green

My Kodak Brownie didn't work
but I have a picture of the green dress.
The film was black and white,
my memory is colour.

We'd eaten our lunch by ten o'clock,
sandwiches and crisps out of paper bags,
the sickly smell inside the coach
as we dizzied through the Dales to Malham.

My first day trip from Hanson Primary School
into a countryside I didn't know.
I don't remember who I sat next to
but it wasn't Wendy Smith in the green dress.

Mr Shepherd led us to Janet's Foss
along a white stone path, the soft curves
of the hills all around me and the blue sky
and the dizziness still inside,

down a rough track to a cool place,
full of ferns and moss and the sound of water.
I didn't know what a waterfall was
or how it could flow into cool deep light.

The stream slid over green, gushing
down into a perfect pool.
I surfaced to sunlight, a green dress
and you, smiling at me.

The Reservoirs of Denshaw

connect to each other, water
flows easily now. We can see
ourselves sharing our lives,
supplying each other's needs.

Victorian pride and precision,
harnessing hillside to an arc
of metal wheels, stonework's
smooth curve, then a skylark

as yellow light begins to fade
and bracken's soft glow covers
our path round the reservoirs.
A curlew calls high above us

as we circle circles of water,
happy here in the secret place
we walk round in our dreams.
Now we sit together and face

hills interlocking like fingers.
Thought of losing this disturbs.
You want to paint it for us both.
I try to hold it here in words.

The Perfect Couple

The Earth pulls the Moon to her.
The closer he gets, the stronger
is the attraction. She wants him
to be part of her. But he wants
his independence and runs around
to preserve space between them.

He feels threatened by a force
that draws him forward so easily.
He fears he will lose his freedom
and strives to keep his distance,
going to the ends of the Earth's
influence on him, to maintain it.

But the Moon does not drift off
or chase after other planets
as he might have done in the past.
He stays. They balance each other
and poised in dynamic equilibrium,
journey through space together,

yet apart. They might not possess
everything, but they are content.
She provides a centre to his life.
He has space and freedom to move.
She likes to have him round her,
to know she is attractive to him,

to know he will remain with her.
He brightens up her dark nights.
She is colourful and full of life.

A FESTIVITY OF LOVE 2

Each of them fills the emptiness
for the other. Their relationship
contains the best of both worlds.

The Contributors

Kate Compston
Kate was born in North Cornwall, now gratefully returned. She is a member of the Indian King Poetry Writers Group, was Selected Poet for Magma 65, and won first prizes in past Hippocrates and Cornwall Contemporary competitions. After working as a United Reformed Church minister and an NHS counsellor, she is now retired, and cares about the E/earth, positive ageing and quietness.

Yvonne Dean
Yvonne has been an artist all her life and also a writer. She enjoys poetry the most, 'the power of distillation and layered thoughts, pegged down like plants to increase themselves'. She is 81 now and says she 'feels so lucky' in her life.

Vicky Edwards
Vicky lives in Bath and is a member of the Endelienta Poetry Group. She has written poetry throughout her adult life for her own creative enjoyment and has used verse together with her illustrations in her children's book, *Following The Fox's Tail*.

Paul S. Fiddes
Paul is a Prebendary of the Collegiate Church of St Endellion, Professor of Systematic Theology in the University of Oxford, and Fellow of the British Academy. He specializes in the relationship between theology and creative literature, his most recent book being *More Things in Heaven and Earth: Shakespeare, Theology, and the Interplay of Texts*.

Victoria Field

Victoria is a writer, poetry therapist and researcher. Her latest collection, *A Speech of Birds* and a memoir of pilgrimage and marriage, *Baggage – A Book of Leavings*, are published by Francis Boutle. After many years in Cornwall, she now lives in Canterbury.

Frances Kent

Frances is a Prebendary of the Collegiate Church of St Endellion, having been for many years Churchwarden of the church. She was born, has lived all her life, and has been a market gardener in the neighbourhood of St Endellion.

Craig Marshall

Craig is a priest in the North Cornwall Cluster of Churches and is a Prebendary of the Collegiate Church of St Endellion. Writing poetry complements his creativity as an artist in mixed media.

John May

John, formerly Rector of St Endellion, St Minver, Port Isaac, St Kew, St Enodoc and St Michael's Porthilly, lives in Tiverton with his wife July and daughter Bee. He enjoys writing, painting and printmaking ... and 'most things in fact'!

Maggie Mealy

Maggie is Cornish and now retired from a mental health career where she used poetry as a facet of therapy. She is a member of the Indian King Poets and is a member of the St Endellion Poetry Group.

Jane Newberry
Jane is a children's writer living in the Tamar Valley. Her play-rhymes *Big Green Crocodile* (Otter-Barry Books) were shortlisted for a CLIPPA award in 2021. In 2022 Jane published her grown-up debut poetry collection *Hoyden's Trove* (Wheelsong Press).

David Penhale
David was born in Port Talbot and raised and educated in Fowey. He is a drama teacher, professional musician, and artist. He has received commendations recently from the Red River Competition, the Poetry Society, and the Charles Causley Competition. His latest collection is *Landfall* (IKP Poets, 2020) and his poems are included in the award-winning anthology, *Cornish Modern Poetries* (Broken Sleep Books, 2022).

Judith Pollinger
Judith is a priest ministering in retirement in the North Cornwall Cluster and a Prebendary Emeritus of the Collegiate Church of St Endellion. She is a member of the Endelienta Poetry Group and has enjoyed writing poetry intermittently throughout her adult life.

Michael Spinks
Michael is a Londoner with a commitment to Cornwall through his friendship with the poet Jack Clemo, whose biography he is writing. He says 'It's the tensions in Clemo's work between faith and emotion that catch attention'. A favourite Clemo uncle moved to Trelights, and makes the link with the magnificent St Endellion Church.

Paul Temme
Paul is a poet and spoken word artist living on the north coast of Cornwall. He is a member of Endelienta Poetry and North Cornwall Stanza and currently studying for an MA in Creative Writing at Plymouth University.

Fay Warne
Fay was born at Whitecross and baptized at Egloshayle, Wadebridge, travelling and learning on her journey. She is grateful to 'Cornwall Mind' for rekindling her interest in poetry. She was recently successful in the Lisa Thomas Prize.

Rowan Williams
Rowan is a former Archbishop of Canterbury, a Prebendary of St Endellion and an Emeritus Fellow of the British Academy. As well as many theological books, he has also had several volumes of poetry published, including *Collected Poems* (Carcanet Poetry, 2021).

Chris Woods
Chris is a retired GP who has more time now to spend with his family, his writing and his piano. He has two poetry collections published, *Recovery* (Enitharmon Press) and *Dangerous Driving* (Comma Press). He is a member of the St Endellion Poetry Group.

Also available:

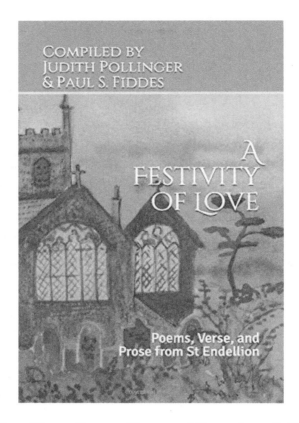

A Festivity of Love. Poems, Verse and Prose from St Endellion, edited by Judith Pollinger and Paul S. Fiddes, Firedint Publishing, Oxford.
Pieces by: Christiana Richardson, Louise Ansdell, Jane Draycott, Paul S. Fiddes, David Foster, Suranjit Gain, Jeff Hankins, Jo Heydon, Helen Jagger, John May, Judith Pollinger, Estelle Price, Christopher Southgate, David Steven, Jenny Swan, Felicity Tattersall, Chris Woods.

Also available:

Loving the Planet. Interfaith Essays on Ecology, Love, and Theology, edited by Paul S. Fiddes, Firedint Publishing, Oxford.
Essays by Jewish, Muslim and Christian scholars:
Emily A. DeMoor, Celia Deane-Drummond, Melissa Raphael, Amir H. Zekrgoo, Leyla H. Tajer, Naftali Rothenberg, Tareq Moqbel, G. O. Marcar, Paul S. Fiddes.

Printed in Great Britain
by Amazon